INFUSED LIQUORS

Part.1

OLEG QUILLED

INFUSED LIQUORS PART.1

by OLEG QUILLED

INTRODUCTION

Infusion is an easy method of making a wide variety of liqueurs. Many of the world's most famous liqueurs are made using this method. Like Angostura bitters, which are also an infusion, there are often closely guarded formulas behind liqueurs, involving an amazing array of herbs and spices.

In spite of the secrecy, though, liqueurs can be easily made in your home distillery. Don't be intimidated by long lists of ingredients; if you've been making bitters or gin using these actual "botanicals" rather than flavorings, you already have a good start.

Liqueurs are simple beasts typically composed of three primary components: base alcohol, flavoring, and sweetener. Mix up those ingredients to your own cacophonous content and you may be rewarded with a bespoke bottle of deliciousness.

You can do this with very little equipment. At a minimum you should have some measuring cups, a small kitchen scale and an alcohol hydrometer for measuring the alcohol by volume (ABV).

Infusions are made by soaking, or infusing, various ingredients in base liquor, often vodka. Infusion times can be anywhere from a couple of days to many weeks. Generally the herbs and spices are infused, and then strained out of the liquid. By definition, liqueurs are sweetened; usually this is done after the botanicals have been infused.

Liqueurs may be sweetened with sugar, sugar syrup, honey or even agave syrup. Here are some recipes for popular liqueurs to get you started.

VODKA

1. **Spicy Garlic-Habanero Vodka**

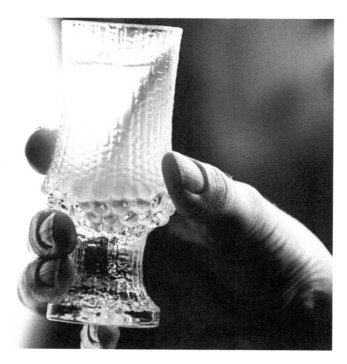

Ingredients

- 1 medium garlic bulb

- 1 habanero pepper

- 1 (750-milliliter) bottle vodka

a) Separate the garlic into cloves and remove the skins.

b) Rinse the habanero pepper to remove any unwanted chemicals. Use the pepper whole or cut it in half, removing all seeds and most of the white flesh.

c) Place the garlic and habanero pepper into a clean quart-sized Mason jar.

d) Fill the jar with vodka. Secure the lid on the jar and shake well.

e) Store the infusion in a cool, dark place for 3 to 5 hours. Taste it after 3 hours, then every 1/2 hour after that until you get the desired flavor.

f) Strain the vodka through a fine-mesh strainer, coffee filter, or cheesecloth and into a separate container. Store as you would any other vodka.

g) Use in your favorite drinks, and enjoy.

2. Lavender-Rosemary Infused Vodka

Ingredients

- 1 (750-milliliter) bottle premium vodka

- 1 sprig fresh rosemary

- 2 sprigs fresh lavender

- Steps to Make It

- Gather the ingredients.

Rinse the herbs and place them into a clean quart-sized Mason jar or similar jar with a tight sealing lid.

Pour the vodka over the herbs and seal the lid tightly.

Shake a few times and store the jar in a cool, dark place for three to five days. Starting on the second day, test the flavor of the infusion daily.

Once the herbal flavor has reached your desired taste, strain the herbs from the vodka using a fine strainer or coffee filter.

Bottle and store as you would any other vodka. Use in your favorite cocktails and enjoy.

3. Raspberry liqueur

- 1-2 lbs. of the best raspberries you can pick or buy
- 1 cup white sugar
- 1 bottle vodka or high-proof alcohol
- 1 sterilized quart canning jar or other glass jar with an airtight lid

a) Boil the canning jar or wash it well, rinse it in warm water, and pour boiling water into it. When the jar has cooled, pour out the water and put in the raspberries. Pour in the sugar and as much vodka as the rest of the jar will hold, leaving an inch or two clearance. Fit the jar with a sterilized canning lid and ring, or some other tight-fitting lid, depending on the jar.

b) Sometimes I put a barrier of plastic wrap between the jar and lid if I am not using a canning jar lid.

c) Put the jar in a dark place, but somewhere where you will see it every other day or so, perhaps near the coffee or tea. Shake the jar every day, or at least a few times a week for a month.

d) The sugar will dissolve gradually, and the color of the liquid will become a lovely red, while the raspberries will turn pale and uninteresting.

e) After the raspberries are almost white, let the jar settle, and carefully pour out the liquid. Some books say the fruit is now wonderful on ice cream, but I find it repulsive and throw it away.

f) NOTE: You can use this recipe for any berry or cherries. Every year I make pie cherry liqueur. Pit the sour cherries, add them to the vodka, and tie the pits in a bit of cheesecloth and add them as well. Some people crack a few of the pits for that almond flavor.

g) Also note that, especially with strawberries, you might get some globs of pectin floating around in the finished product. They are harmless but look disgusting. Filter them out when they form. I've never tried it, but it might be interesting to see if mashing the strawberries and adding half a teaspoon of pectic enzyme for twelve hours before adding the sugar and alcohol would help.

h) Taste the liqueur. If you want it sweeter, boil another $\frac{1}{2}$ to 1 cup of sugar with half the amount of water, cool it, and add in increments, tasting as you go. You will find that this procedure makes you quite cheerful.

i) I now filter the liqueur through a paper coffee filter, probably losing some alcohol content as I go, but that's life. You can also use several thicknesses of clean cheesecloth.

j) Store the liqueur in another jar or pretty bottle that has been cleaned and rinsed out with boiling water. Make sure the lid is tight. Keep in the dark to maintain the color.

4.   Orange liqueur

- 1 pint dried orange and tangerine peels
- 1 cup sugar
- 1 bottle vodka
- 1 quart jar

a) Boil the canning jar or wash it well, rinse it in warm water, and pour boiling water into it. When the jar has cooled, pour out the water and put in the orange peels. Pour in the sugar and as much vodka as the rest of the jar will hold, leaving an inch or two clearance. Fit the jar with a sterilized canning lid and ring, or some other tight-fitting lid, depending on the jar.

b) Sometimes I put a barrier of plastic wrap between the jar and the lid if I am not using a canning jar lid.

c) Put the jar in a dark place, but somewhere where you will see it every other day or so. Shake the jar every day, or at least a few times a week for a month.

d) The sugar will dissolve gradually, and the color of the liquid will become a pale orange. It will take several months to leach the flavor out of the peels. Taste it once in a while to see how it's doing. There is likely to be a very firm layer of pectin on the bottom of the jar. Ignore it.
e) Let the jar settle, and carefully pour out the liquid.
f) Taste the liqueur. If you want it sweeter, boil another $\frac{1}{2}$ to 1 cup of sugar with half the amount of water, cool it, and add in increments, tasting as you go.
g) Filter the liqueur through a paper coffee filter or use several thicknesses of clean cheesecloth.
h) Store the liqueur in another jar or pretty bottle that has been cleaned and rinsed out with boiling water. Make sure the lid is tight. Keep in the dark to maintain the color.

i) This liqueur is infinitely useful. I make this with Everclear and use it for orange flavoring in cookies and cakes.

5. Watermelon Vodka

Ingredients

- 1 (750-milliliter) bottle vodka

- 1 small watermelon, cubed

- Steps to Make It

- Gather the ingredients.

In a clean, quart-sized infusion jar with a tight seal, place the cubed watermelon.

Pour the vodka over the fruit and shake a few times.

Seal the lid and store the jar in a cool, dark place for 4 to 6 days. Shake it once or twice a day. Beginning on the third day, test the flavor of the infusion daily.

Once the watermelon flavor is to your taste, strain the watermelon from the vodka. You may need to strain twice or use a cheesecloth to remove all of the fruit and seeds.

Wash the jar and return the flavored vodka to it. Store as you would any other vodka.

Mix the watermelon vodka into cocktails and enjoy.

6.   Nut liqueur

- 2 lbs. fresh, unsalted, unblanched almonds, chopped OR the same amount of filberts or hazelnuts (though be sure they are fresh!)
- 1 cup sugar
- 1 bottle vodka or brandy
- 1 half-gallon jar or 2 quart jars

a) Rinse the jar out with boiling water.
b) Put the chopped nuts in the jar, and add the sugar and the vodka or brandy. Shake daily for a month or more until fragrant, then strain off the nuts, and add sugar syrup if desired. The color will be brown or tan. Filter or stand to clear. Nuts have oil in them, and so this will, too—it won't keep as long as fruit will, but it is quite nice to have around. Don't invite any squirrels over.

7. Banana Liqueur

- 2 medium-sized ripe bananas

- 3 cups vodka

- 1 teaspoon pure vanilla extract

- 1 cup sugar

- 1 cup water

Peel and mash the bananas. Combine banana, vodka, and vanilla extract in a jar; mix well. Cover tightly and let steep in a cool, dark place for 1 week. When steeping period is complete, strain and filter the liquid.

Combine sugar and water in a heavy saucepan. Bring to boil over medium heat. Reduce heat and simmer until sugar has completely dissolved, about 3 minutes. Remove from heat and let cool to room temperature.

Combine sugar syrup, mave, and the filtered liquid. Pour into bottles and cap tighly. Let age at least 1 month before serving.

8. Anisette(Licorice Liqueur)

- 2 tablespoons crushed star anise

- 3 cups vodka

- 2 cups sugar

- 1 cup water

Combine crushed star anise and vodka in a jar. Cover tightly and let steep in a cool, dark place for 2 weeks. When steeping period is complete, strain and filter the liquid.

Combine sugar and water in a heavy saucepan. Bring to a boil over medium heat. Resuce haeat and simmer until sugare has completely dissolved, about 3 minutes. Remove from heat and let cool to room temperature.

Combine sugare syrup and filtered vodka mixture. Pour into bottles and cap tightly. Let age at least one month before serving.

9. Plum Liqueur

- 1 pound fresh, purple plums (Santa Rosa preferred)

- 2 cups vodka

- 1 cup sugar

- 1 1-inch cinnamon stick cup water

- 4 whole cloves

Pit plums and cut plums into 1-inch chunks. Combine plums, sugar, cinnamon sticks, cloves and vodka in a large jar. Mix well. Cover tightly and let steep in a cool, dark place for 2 months. Shake jar occasionally.

When steeping period is complete, strain and filter the liquid.

Pour into bottles and cap tightly. Let age at least 1 month before serving.

10. Tangerine Liqueur

- 6 Tangerines

- 2 cups vodka or brandy

- $\frac{1}{2}$ cup sugar

- $\frac{3}{4}$ cup water

Using a swivel blade peeler, peel tangerines, scraping off peel only, avoiding the white membrane. Place peels in a jar with the vodka or brandy. Cover tightly and let steep in a cool, dark place for 3 weeks. Shake jar occasionally.

When steeping period is complete, strain and filter the liquid.

Combine sugar and water in a heavy saucepan. Bring to a boil over medium heat. Reduce heat and simmer until sugar has completely dissolved, about 3 minutes. Remove from heat and let cool to room temperature.

Combine sugar syrup with the filtered liquid. Pour into bottles and cap tightly. Let age at least 1 month.

11. Allspice Liqueur

- 3/4 tsp. allspice [presumably ground]
- 1 1/2 cups vodka or brandy
- 1/2 cup sugar syrup

Steep allspice in alcohol for 10 days. Strain and filter. Add syrup. Mature for 1-6 months.

12. Lavender Liqueur

- 6 Tbsp Dried Lavender Petals

- 1 Fifth 80-Proof Vodka

- 1 Cup Sugar Syrup

a) Steep the petals inthe vodka for one week. Filter through cheesecloth and squeeze the petals to extract as much liquid as possible.

b) Add the sugar syrup and enjoy.

13. Green Tea Liqueur

- 6 tsp. green tea leaves (loose, good quality)

- 3 c. vodka

- 1 c. syrup

- 2-3 drops green food colouring

The tea leaves should be steeped in the vodka for only 24 hours; longer makes the liqueur bitter. Shake the jar or bottle well when you add the leaves. Add the sweetener and colouring the next day.

14. Cinnamon liqueur

Ingredient

- 1 Cinnamon stick

- Cloves

- 1 teaspoon Ground coriander seed

- 1 cup Vodka

- $\frac{1}{2}$ cup Brandy

- $\frac{1}{2}$ cup Sugar syrup (see recipe)

Steep all herbs in alcohol for 2 weeks. Strain and filter until clear and add sugar syrup to taste. Let stand 1 week and its ready to serve. Makes a nice hot drink when added to boiling water.

15. Vanilla-coffee liqueur

Ingredient

- 1½ cup Brown sugar; packed

- 1 cup Granulated sugar

- 2 cups Water

- ½ cup Instant coffee powder

- 3 cups Vodka

- ½   Vanilla bean; split (or 2 teaspoons vanilla extract)

Combine sugars and water. Boil for 5 minutes. Gradually stir in coffee.

Cool. Add vodka and vanilla and mix thoroughly. Cover and let ripen for 1 month. Remove vanilla bean.

16. Fresh mint liqueur

Ingredient

- 1¼ cupFresh mint leaves, slightly packed *

- 3 cupsVodka

- 2 cupsGranulated sugar

- 1 cup Water

- 1 teaspoon   Glycerin

- 8 drops   Green food coloring (opt)

- 2 drops   Blue food coloring (opt)

Wash leaves in cold water several times. Shake or pat dry gently. Snip each leaf in half or thirds. Discard stems. measure cut mint leaves, packing lightly.

Combine mint leaves and vodka in aging container. Cap and let stand in a cool place for 2 weeks, shaking occasionally.

After initial aging, strain leaves from liqueur; discard leaves.

In a saucepan, combine sugar and water. Bring to a boil, stirring constantly. Let cool. Add cooled syrup to liqueur base, stirring to combine. Add glycerin and food color; pour into aging container for secondary aging of 1-3 more months.

A real good aging container is $\frac{1}{2}$ gallon canning jars. If you want more of this get the book " Classic Liqueurs;

The Art of Making and Cooking with Liqueurs " by Cheryl Long and Heather Kibbey.

17. Fresh orange liqueur

Ingredient

- 3 cups Vodka

- 3   Whole sweet oranges, cut into wedges

- ½   Lemon

- 2   Whole cloves

- 1 cup Basic sugar syrup*

Prep time: 15 mins Cook time: 0 mins Difficulty: **
Source: Gourmet Gifts By Dona Z. Meilach *To make
basic sugar syrup, combine 1 cup sugar with ½ cup water
in a saucepan. Bring to a boil over high heat and stir until

all the sugar is dissolved and the mixture is clear. Cool before using. Makes 1 cup.

In a wide - mouth jar, pour the vodka over the oranges, lemon and cloves so that the vodka completely covers the fruit. Seal tightly and let sit in a cool, dark place for 10 days. Strain through a paper coffee filter and discard the solids. Add sugar syrup. With a funnel, pour the liqueur into gift bottles and close tightly with corks or screw - on caps. Let sit for 3 to 4 weeks before using.

18. Strawberries with limoncello

Ingredient

- 30   Fresh strawberries cut into halves

- 4 teaspoons Limoncello liqueur; (20ml)

- Freshly ground pepper; sprinkled after

- ; taste

- 4 teaspoons Freshly squeezed orangg juice; (20ml)

Cut strawberries and put in a big bowl.

Add the orange juice, the liqueur and freshly ground prpper. Leave to marinate for at least 30 minutes.

Serve as it is, if wanted with Italian biscuits.

19. Fruit compote pie

Ingredient

- 1   9" pie crust

- 1 cup Dried apricots, chopped

- 1 cup Dried peaches and/or apples,

- Chopped

- 6 ounces   Apricot or peach nectar

- ¼ cup Peach or apricot liqueur

- 2 tablespoons   Dried cranberries, cherries

- Or raisins

- 1 cup Sour cream
- 1   Egg
- ⅓ cup Sugar
- 2 tablespoons   Flour
- ½ teaspoon Grated lemon peel
- pinch Nutmeg
- ½ cup Flour
- ⅓ cup Brown sugar, firmly packed
- ½ teaspoon   Cinnamon
- ¼ cup Unsalted butter, melted
- ¼ cup Pecans or walnuts, chopped

Prepare pie crust and crimp. chill at least 15 minutes.

Bring apricots, peaches, nectar and liqueur to a boil; reduce heat and simmer 10 minutes. Stir in cranberries and continue to cook until fruit is soft and liquid is absorbed. Remove from heat and let stand while preparing rest of pie.

Preheat oven to 425F.

Sour Cream Batter:

Combine all ingredients until well blended; blend with filling and spoon into pie shell.

Crumb Topping:

Combine and scatter in an even layer on top of the filling.

Bake pie 15 minutes; reduce heat to 350F. and continue baking 20 to 25 minutes until crumbs are golden brown and filling is almost set.

Serve at room temperature.

20. Fruit-nut balls with liqueur

Ingredient

- 1 cup   Chopped dates

- 1½ cup Seedless raisins

- ½ cup Dried apricots

- 1 cup   Black walnuts -- chopped

- 2 cups Graham cracker crumbs

- ½ cup Southern Comfort

- ⅓ cup Honey

- 1 teaspoon   Orange peel -- grated

- 1 dash Salt

- 1 cup Dried coconut

1. Put fruit, nuts and graham cracker crumbs through food processor or food chopper using the finest blade.

2. Mix together the honey, liqueur, orange peel and salt; add to fruit mixture. Mix well with hands and shape into marble-sized balls. Roll in the coconut.

3. Store in tightly covered container. Need not be refrigerated but store in a container with a tight-fitting lid.

21. Hot buttered cider

Ingredient

- 1 quart   Apple cider, preferably

- Freshly pressed

- ¼ cup Light corn syrup

- 2 tablespoons   Unsalted butter

- 2   Cinnamon sticks

- 3   Whole cloves

- 2 slices   Lemon

- 6 ounces   Apple liqueur

In a large saucepan, combine the cider, corn syrup, butter, cinnamon sticks, cloves and lemon slices.

Heat over a moderately low flame until the cider is hot and the butter is melted. Remove from the heat.

While the cider is heating, pour one ounce of liqueur into each of 6 mugs or heatproof glasses. Pour the hot cider into the mugs and serve at once.

22. Instant raspberry cordial jam

Ingredient

- 12 ounces   Raspberry jam

- 1 tablespoon To 2 Chambord or other

- Raspberry liqueur

Stir liqueur into jam; cover and refrigerate at least one day to allow flavors to meld.

23. Peppermint schnapps liqueur

Ingredient

- ⅓ cup Granulated sugar

- 1   Bottle; (16 oz) Light corn syrup

- 2 cups 80 proof vodka

- 2 teaspoons Peppermint extract

1. Combine sugar and corn syrup in a 2 quart pan over medium heat. Heat until sugar dissolve, stirring regularly (about 5 minutes) 2. When sugar has dissolved, add vodka and stir well. Remove mixture from heat and cover

tightly with lid. Let cool. 3. Add peppermint extract to mixture and pour into a sealable bottle.

Makes 4 cups.

24. Lime liqueur

Ingredient

- 2   Dozen limes
- ½ teaspoon   Ground cinnamon
- 6   Cloves
- 2 pounds   White sugar
- 6 cups 80 proof vodka
- 2 cups Water
- Green food dye

Wash limes. Slice each lime into 5 or 6 slices. Combine with cinnamon, cloves, vodka, water, and white sugar. Shake well until sugar is dissolved. Cover. Set in cool place for two weeks. Strain through fine sieve and leave alone to clear. Decant, pouring clear liquid into bottles. Tint a very very pale green color.

25. Liqueur & orange stuffing

Ingredient

- 18 ounces Package stuffing mix

- $\frac{3}{4}$ cup Butter

- 1 large Onion, finely chopped

- 1 cup Celery, minced

- $\frac{1}{2}$ cup Raisins

- $\frac{1}{2}$ cup Mandarin Orange Sections, chopped

- $\frac{1}{4}$ cup Sabra or Grand Marnier Orange Liqueur

- $\frac{3}{4}$ cup Hot water

- 1 Egg, beaten

(This recipe is for a 10-12 lb bird. Increase measurements for larger size.) Heat butter to foam. Add onion and celery, stirring in butter until wilted. Remove from heat and stir in stuffing, mixing along with the raisins, chopped orange sections, liqueur, hot water and egg. Spoon loosely into the bird's chest cavity.

26. Spicy herbal liqueur

Ingredient

- 6   Cardamom pods*

- 3 teaspoons Anise seeds*

- $2\frac{1}{4}$ teaspoon Chopped angelica root*

- 1   Cinnamon stick

- 1   Clove

- $\frac{1}{4}$ teaspoon   Mace

- 1   Fifth of vodka

- 1 cup Sugar syrup (see recipe)

- Container: 1/2 gallon jar

Remove seeds from cardomom pods. Add the anise seeds, and crush all the kernals with the back of a fork. Put them in a 1-quart container adding angelica root, cinnamon stick, clove, mace, and vodka. Shake mixture well and store in a cupboard for 1 week. Pour through cheesecloth lined strainer several times. Blend the liquid with the sugar syrup. Ready to serve. *Most of these ingredients can be found at health food stores. This liqueur is similiar to Italian Strega and the spicy taste may not appeal to everyone.

27. Pineapple grand marnier

Ingredient

- 1 large   Glass container with a lid

- 1   Sweet pineapple peeled; cored and sliced

- 1   Bottle vodka; 750 ml

- $2\frac{1}{2}$ ounce   Pineapple infused vodka

- $\frac{3}{4}$ ounce   Grand Marnier

- Orange peel

To infuse the vodka. Place an entire ripe pineapple, peeled, cored, and sliced, in a glass container and cover with a bottle of vodka. Refrigerate pineapple for at least 48 hours.

To assemble the drink. Pour $2\frac{1}{2}$ ounces of pineapple infused vodka and $\frac{3}{4}$ ounces of Grand Marnier in cocktail shaker filled with ice.

Shake vigorously and strain into a chilled martini glass.

Garnish with orange peel.

28. Raspberry infused vodka martini

Ingredient

- 1.00   Twenty-five oz bottle vodka

- 1.00 pint   Raspberries; plus some for

- Garnish

- 6.00 ounce   Cointreau

Pour 1 bottle of vodka into a jar and add 1 pint of fresh raspberries. Let stand for 3 days Into a martini shaker, add 2 ounces raspberryinfused vodka, $\frac{1}{2}$ ounce Cointreau and ice. Shake, then strain into martini glass. Garnish with raspberries.

29. Papaya liqueur

Ingredient

- 1 Papaya

- 1 cup Vodka

- 1 small Lemon wedge, scraped peel

- $\frac{1}{4}$ cup Sugar syrup, optional to taste (see recipe)

Look for medium-sized papaya (slightly larger than a pear) with smooth, unbruised skin, and a fruity aroma. Best time is May and June. Dark spots on the skin are a bad sign and will cause a bad flavor (check stem for decay and softness). Cut papaya in half, remove seeds, and peel skin. Cut in medium chunks and place in vodka with lemon peel(twist to release flavor). Let steep for 1 week.

Strain and squeeze fruit, extracting juice. If desired, add sugar syrup. Store for 3 weeks

30. Blueberry liqueur

Ingredient

- 3 cupsFresh blueberries or blackberries

- 1 eachClove

- $\frac{1}{2}$ cup Sugar syrup (see recipe) to taste

- 2 cups Vodka

- 1 each Lemon vedge, scraped peel

Note: Blueberries can be bought in season(May to Sept). Avoid stained baskets and DO NOT rinse until ready to use. If freezing, do so BEFORE rinsing. Rinse with cold water. Rinse berries and lightly crush. Add vodka, lemon peel, and clove. Pour in DARK bottle and store for 3-4 months. Strain through dampened cheesecloth squeezing out as much juice as possible. Add sugar syrup to taste and store another 4 weeks. Liqueur will tend to be on the watery side. Try adding glycerine if a thicker consistency is desired. Good for baking.

31. Chocolate liqueur

Ingredient

- 2 teaspoons Pure chocolate extract

- $\frac{1}{2}$ teaspoon   Pure vanilla extract

- $1\frac{1}{2}$ cup Vodka

- $\frac{1}{2}$ cup Sugar syrup (see recipe)

- $\frac{1}{2}$ teaspoon   Fresh mint (optional)

- drop Peppermint extract(optional)

Mix all ingredients and let mature 2 weeks. The chocolate tends to settle on the bottom and may need to be stirred before serving.

Finished version will tend to be thin, but is still quite tasty and excellent for mixing in coffee or pouring over desserts. Add glycerine to thicken if desired. For chocolate mint, add $\frac{1}{2}$ teaspoon fresh mint and a few drops of peppermint extract. Let mature 2 additional weeks.

32. Coconut liqueur

Ingredient

- 2 cups Packaged coconut

- 4   Coriander seeds

- $\frac{1}{4}$ teaspoon   Vanilla extract

- 3 cups Vodka

- $\frac{1}{2}$ cup Brandy

Add all ingredients together and steep for 3-4 weeks.
Turn jar every few days. The coconut tends to be porous
and absorbs the alcohol so be sure to thoroughly strain
and filter the mixture to yield the largest amount.

Natural coconut may also be used, but tends to be watery and requires more coconut.

33. Curacao liqueur

Ingredient

- 3 tablespoons Bitter orange peel

- Dozen valencia or navel

- Oranges

- 2⅔ cup 80 proof vodka

- 1⅓ cup Water

- 2 cups White sugar

- 12 Whole cloves

- 1 teaspoon   Ground cinnamon

- 2 teaspoons Whole corriander seeds

Peel oranges. Section and cut each section into halves. Put into the mixing jar along with the bitter orange peel, cloves, corriander and cinnamon. Add sugar, vodka, and water. Shake vigorously until the sugar is dissolved. Leave to infuse for 5 weeks. Strain and leave to clear. Be patient because this takes longer than most liqueurs. When clear, decant off clear liqueur and bottle.

34. Grapefruit liqueur

Ingredient

- 6 Medium or large grapefruit
- 3 cups 80 proof vodka
- 1 cup Water
- 2 tablespoons Whole corriander seed
- 1 teaspoon   Ground cinnamon
- 4 cups White sugar

Cut or scrape off zest, yellow part of rind. Then peel grapefruit and discard pith or white part. Separate grapefruit sections and cut each section into several pieces. Combine the rest of the ingredients.

Cover. Leave to infuse for several weeks. Strain and let the liqueur clear for a week to 10 days. Carefully pour off the clear liqueur. If desired, a small amount of yellow food dye may be added for a stronger yellow color.

35. Honey liqueur

Ingredient

- 2 cups Vodka or brandy

- $\frac{3}{4}$ pounds Honey

- 3 tablespoons Orange rind, or 1/2 the

- Peel of an orange

- 1 cup Water, warm but not boiling

- 1 Clove

- 2 Cinnamon sticks, 2 inches each

Peel the orange find in one long spiral if possible, particularly if you want an attractive presentation. Disolve the honey in the water and add to the vodka and spices in an attractive bottle with the orange peel.

Let stand, well corked shaking every few days. I like the flavor well developed, and do not usually strain it at all, but check it after 2 or 3 weeks, and if you don't want too strong an orange spice flavor, strain the peel and spices out and rebottle.

36. Tea liqueur

Ingredient

- 2 teaspoons Black tea leaves*

- $1\frac{1}{2}$ cup Vodka

- $\frac{1}{2}$ cup Sugar syrup (see recipe)

Steep the tea leaves in vodka for 24 hours - NOT longer as a bitter taste will occur. Strain and add sugar syrup. Age for 2 weeks. *Your favorite tea may be used for the flavor you desire and spices can be added as well.

37. Peppermint liqueur

Ingredient

- 2 teaspoons Peppermint extract(or 3 ts)

- 3 cupsVodka

- 1 cup Sugar syrup

Combine all ingredients and stir. Let stand for 2 weeks.
Use 3 teaspoons of extract for a stronger mint taste
and additional sugar syrup for a sweeter thicker liqueur.

38. Angelica liqueur

Ingredient

- 3 tablespoons   Dried chopped angelica root

- 1 tablespoon Chopped almonds

- 1   Allspice berry, cracked

- 1   1" piece cinnamon stick, broken

- 3   To 6 anise or fennel seeds, crushed

- $\frac{1}{8}$ teaspoon   Powdered coriander seed
- 1 tablespoon Chopped fresh marjoram leaves or 1 tsp. dried
- $1\frac{1}{2}$ cup Vodka
- $\frac{1}{2}$ cup Granulated sugar
- $\frac{1}{4}$ cup Water
- 1 drop Each yellow and green food color,(optional)

Combine all herbs, nuts and spices with vodka in a 1 quart or larger aging container. Cap tightly and shake daily for 2 weeks. Strain through a fine muslin cloth or coffee filter; discarding solids. Clean out aging container. Place liquid back in container.

Place sugar and water in saucepan and stir to combine over medium heat.** When sugar is completely dissolved, set aside and let cool. When cool combine with food coloring and add to liqueur liquid. Cap and allow to age and mellow in a cool, dark place for one month.

39. Blueberries with orange liqueur

Ingredient

- 1 cup Orange flavored liqueur

- 1 cup Water

- 1 cup Sugar

- $1\frac{1}{2}$ pounds Fresh blueberries

- 20 Fresh lavender flower heads

Prepare jars, lids and boiling water bath. Combine the liqueur, water and sugar in a pan and cook over med-high heat, stirring frequently, until sugar is dissolved and mixture has come to boil. Remove from heat.

Pick over, wash and dry blueberries, then pack them in hot dry jars, placing 4 lavender flower heads in each jar. Leave $\frac{1}{2}$ inch headspace. Pour hot liquid into jars, just covering berries. Wipe rims with clean towel and attach lids securely.

Place jars in boiling water bath, and when water returns to full boil, process for 15 mins.

40. Seed liqueur

- 4 tablespoons anise or caraway seeds, bruised or half ground
- 1 cup sugar
- 1 bottle vodka or brandy
- 1 quart jar

a) Put the seeds into a clean jar that has been rinsed out with boiling water. Add the sugar and the vodka or brandy. Shake daily for a month or more until fragrant, then strain off the seeds, and add sugar syrup if desired. The color will be tan. Filter or stand to clear.

41.   Apple liqueur

- 2-3 lbs. tart/sweet flavorful apples
- 1 cup sugar
- 1 bottle vodka or brandy
- 1 half-gallon jar

a) Wash and core the apples, but don't remove the peel. Chop them finely. Rinse out the jar with boiling water. Add the sugar and the brandy and fit the jar with a lid. Shake every day for one to two months. Sometimes the peel will give it a rosy tint.

b) Strain out the fruit, filter, and add sugar syrup to taste. This also might develop a pectin haze, so be sure to filter.

42. Apricot or peach liqueur

- 1-2 lbs. dead-ripe apricots or peaches
- 1 cup sugar
- 1 bottle brandy or vodka
- 1 half-gallon jar or 2 quart jars

a) Wash and pit the apricots. Rinse the jar out with boiling water, add the apricots or peaches, sugar, and alcohol. Cover and shake once a day or so for one to two months. Strain and filter, then sweeten to taste with sugar syrup. These fruits are also nice lightly spiced with whole spices. Some people like to add a couple of the cracked pits to the fruit during soaking.

43. Coffee vanilla liqueur

- 2 ozs. good instant coffee
- 2 cups sugar
- 4 ozs. really good vanilla (do not use imitation vanilla)
- 1-2 Madagascar or Tahitian vanilla beans (optional)
- 1 bottle brandy or vodka

a) Rinse the jar out with boiling water. Drain.
b) Heat the water, coffee, and the sugar to simmer. Remove from the heat and cool. If you are using the vanilla beans, chop them fine, losing none of the black inner seeds, and put them in the jar. Add the 4 ounces of vanilla. Pour in the coffee/sugar/water and stir. After two to three months, strain out the vanilla beans. Bottle. You might want to add more sugar.
c) A tablespoon or two of this in chocolate cookies, cake batter, or icing is a wonderful addition. It doesn't overwhelm the chocolate but instead gives it more depth.

d) You can pour some rum or brandy over the vanilla beans after you have removed them; you will get more flavor out of them if you let them stand for another few months.

44. Sugar-shine

- 6 gallons (23 L) unchlorinated or filtered water
- 14 pounds (6.4 kg) granulated white sugar
- 1 package Turbo yeast (enough for at least 6 gallons wash)

a) In a large stock pot or mashing pot (at least 4-gallon capacity), bring 2 gallons of water to a boil. Turn off heat, add the sugar and stir to dissolve. Put 3 gallons of cold water in a fermenting bucket (8 gallons or larger), then pour in the hot water and sugar mixture. Stir to combine. Check temperature; you are aiming for about 38°C/100°F. Add more warm or cold water until there is a total of 6.6 gallons liquid (25 liters). Check temperature again. If it is over 38°C/100°F, just put the fermenter lid on loosely and let it cool down a bit. Check the specific gravity and record this number.

b) Add the yeast and stir vigorously until the yeast and nutrients are dissolved. Put on the lid, add the airlock and let it ferment at room temperature.

c) Depending on conditions, fermentation times can vary, so remember to watch the airlock for bubbling. Once the bubbling slows down noticeably, start checking the specific gravity once a day.

d) Once fermentation is complete, check and records the specific gravity.

e) Transfer the wash to the still with a siphon, leaving behind as much yeast sediment as possible. Record the volume of wash in the still and estimated alcohol content.

f) Distill in a column still.

45. Wheat Vodka

- 6 gallons (23 L) filtered or unchlorinated water
- 1½ teaspoons (7.5 ml) gypsum
- 8½ pounds (3.9 kg) flaked wheat
- 2.2 pounds (1 kg) wheat malt, crushed
- 1 package whiskey yeast/enzyme combination
- Have two large (at least 8-gallon capacity) fermenting buckets on hand.

a) Pour all the water into a large stockpot; I use my stainless steel 10-gallon mashing pot for this. Heat the water to 71°C/160°F. Stir in the gypsum, and then add the flaked wheat. Stir until the grain begins to liquefy; it will look something like oatmeal. The temperature will drop when you add the grain, so check it again. If it is below 67°C/152°F, heat gently until the temperature is between 67°–68°C/152°–155°F. Be sure to stir while it is heating. If the temperature is above 68°C/155°F, stop and let it cool until it is 68°C/155°F.

b) Add the wheat malt, stirring to incorporate. Put the lid on the pot and let the mash rest for 60 minutes. Stir gently and check the temperature every 15 minutes or so; it should stay at 65°C/149°F or above. After 60 minutes, use the iodine test to check for starch conversion. If conversion isn't complete, replace the lid and let rest another 30 minutes.

c) Let the mash cool to 32°C/90°F. Take a sample of the clear liquid on top of the mash and test the specific gravity. Record this number; it should be about 1.060 to 1.065 (remember to correct for temperature). Transfer mash, with the grain, to a fermenting bucket. Pour the mash vigorously back and forth between the two buckets several times to aerate the mash. Add the yeast, put the lid and airlock on the fermenter, and let ferment in a warm place until fermentation is done.

d) Strain the grains from the mash using a large straining bag. (See chapter 8 for information on feeding the mashed grains to your poultry or other livestock.) Let the strained liquid stand for several hours or overnight to let the yeast sediment settle.

e) Siphon the wash to the still. Be sure to record the volume of liquid, specific gravity and estimated alcohol content of the wash. Distill at least 3 times, starting with a stripping run.

46. Aquavit

- 50 ounces (1.5 L) good-quality vodka
- 3 tablespoons (45 ml) caraway seed
- 2 tablespoons (30 ml) cumin seed
- 2 tablespoons (30 ml) dill seed
- 1 tablespoon (15 ml) fennel seed
- 1 tablespoon (15 ml) coriander seed
- 2 whole star anise

- 3 whole cloves
- Peel of $\frac{1}{2}$ organic lemon, cut in strips
- Peel of $\frac{1}{2}$ organic orange, cut in strips
- 1 ounce (30 ml) simple syrup (optional)

a) Preheat your oven to 204°C/400°F. Toast the seeds on a foil-lined cookie sheet for 6 to 8 minutes; stir 2 or 3 times while they are toasting. Remove from oven and let cool briefly. Crush seeds lightly in a mortar and pestle, then put them in a large infusion jar (a half-gallon Mason jar works well). Add the star anise, cloves, lemon and orange peel, then the vodka. Add a bit more vodka if needed to completely cover the other ingredients. Seal tightly with a lid and shake briefly.

b) Infuse at room temperature for not less than 2 weeks. Shake the jar every 2 days while infusing. Strain, first through a strainer, then through cheesecloth or a coffee filter. Add the simple syrup, if using, and bottle. Best stored in the freezer.

c) Making citron (lemon) vodka is easy and quick.

47. Citron Vodka

- 1 bottle (750 ml) filtered vodka
- $\frac{1}{4}$ cup (60 ml) dried organic lemon peel

a) Peel of 3 fresh organic lemons, cut in thin strips, with no pith

b) In a half-gallon Mason jar, pour vodka over lemon peel and fresh rind. Cover and let macerate for 2 days. Smell and taste and strain out lemon rind as soon as the flavor and aroma suit your taste. Perfect for making the quintessential Cosmopolitan

c) If you plan to use dried citrus peel frequently, I suggest buying it in quantity. I get organic lemon, lime and orange peel by the pound at very reasonable prices from Starwest Botanicals (see Resources). For small quantities, though, it can be more cost-effective to make your own. It also gives you the choice of different types of fruit, especially with oranges, which can have bitter or sweet peel.

d) It's always best to buy organic citrus fruits when you plan to use the peel. Preheat your oven to its lowest setting. Using a vegetable peeler or sharp paring knife, cut thin strips of peel. Try to avoid cutting into the white pith. Cut the strips into small pieces, about $\frac{1}{4}$" by $\frac{1}{2}$". It's more important that the pieces be fairly uniform in size, so don't worry about the size too much. Spread the pieces on a baking sheet in one layer. Put the sheet in the oven and bake until the peel has shrunk noticeably; if you see the edges of the pieces starting to brown, take the sheet out of the oven. Depending on the temperature in your oven, this can take anywhere from 5 minutes to 20 minutes or so. The peel will continue to dry once it's out of the oven, so put the baking sheet on a cooling rack and let it sit until the peel feels dry. It can be used right away or stored in an airtight jar.

e) Did you know that there actually isn't all that much difference between gin and vodka? The main thing that makes gin different is that, at one point in the distillation, a special basket containing juniper berries and various herbs and spices is placed in the still. As the spirit begins to vaporize, the steam rises up through the basket, infusing the spirit with the familiar juniper tang of gin. Without this extra step, gin would smell and taste pretty much like one more vodka.

TEQUILA

48. Lemongrass-Ginger Infused Tequila

Ingredients

- 2 stalks fresh lemongrass

- 1 large piece fresh ginger

- 1 (750-milliliter) bottle blanco tequila

a) Peel the outer leaves from the lemongrass stalks, cut off the ends, and chop the remaining grass into thin rounds.

b) Place the lemongrass and whole ginger in the bottom of a clean quart-sized jar with a tight sealing lid.

c) Pour the tequila over the herbs and shake a few times.

d) Seal the lid tight and store the jar in a cool, dark place for about 2 weeks. Test the flavor of the infusion every day, beginning on the fifth day.

e) Once the flavor is to taste, strain the lemongrass and ginger from the tequila.

f) Wash the jar and return the flavored tequila to it. Store as you would any other tequila.

g) Use the infused tequila in cocktails, and enjoy.

49. Tequila (Agave Spirit)

- 2 bottles (44 oz. each) organic blue agave syrup
- 2 gallons (7.6 L) warm water, filtered or unchlorinated
- 1 package whiskey yeast/enzyme combination

a) Put 1 gallon of warm water in a fermenting bucket. Add the agave syrup and stir to dissolve. Stir in the second gallon of water. Check and record the specific gravity; it should be around 1.065 to 1.070. Make sure the temperature of the wash is 29°-33°C/85°-92°F and add the yeast. Put the lid and airlock in place and ferment.

b) Transfer the wash to your still and do a stripping run. Then do a spirit run on the low wines, distilling until the accumulated hearts are about 55% ABV.

50. Margarita liqueur

Ingredient

- 1 Bottle silver tequila

- 1 Peel of orange; cut in continuous spiral

- 1 Peel of lime; cut in continuous spiral

- 6 ounces Cointreau

Share a shot of tequila with a friend while making this. Add citrus peel to tequila remaining in bottle, and then add the Cointreau to taste. Keep refrigerated and serve in sherry glasses. Remove citrus peel if liqueur starts to become bitter. It can be served straight or on the rocks with a twist of orange peel.

Take a bottle of this to the host of a dinner party instead of a bottle of wine.

CONCLUSION

Your new bespoke liqueur can be drunk now but will improve if you let it sit in the bottle for 2-3 months. The flavors will meld together, and the alcoholic edges will smooth out.

Making liqueurs is a lot of fun and there are worlds of possibility within them. Hopefully this eBook has empowered you with enough basic information to get started. And remember to share your creations with friends when the trials of isolation are over! Cheers!